Breathe:
This Too Shall Pass!

Ronda Knuth

For information write: Ronda Knuth, 11913 W. 13th Ave., Lakewood, CO 80401

Breathe: This Too Shall Pass!

Knuth, Ronda.

ISBN – 13: 978-1515188469

ISBN – 10: 1515188469

DEDICATION

Dedicated to

Erna May Hunter

My Mother, My Friend

December 5, 1932 — November 24, 2011

CONTENTS

Previously Published by Ronda Knuth

When Memory Fades:

Sunrise Stories of Real People

© 2014 Ronda Knuth

ISBN-13: 978-1496142054

ISBN-10: 1496142055

FOREWORD

Ronda Knuth asked me to write a foreword for this book before I saw it. Having now gone through it, I would in any case have volunteered for this privilege. I want to go on record as urging all Christians to read what Ronda Knuth has written from her heart.

Ronda has captured the isolation that so many of us feel in life's experiences, and reminded us we are not alone. We can take the encouragement of this book, and find a resolve, that can lead us through the circumstances that seem to overwhelm us.

I have had the wonderful opportunity to know Ronda through the years as her pastor and I can share with confidence that she writes with compassion, integrity, and thoughtfulness.

Breathe: This Too Shall Pass will bring hope to all who read it and strength to all who apply it to their lives. Ronda has a profound and unique insight into life's challenges and how the Word of God is more than a source of inspiration, but a guiding light of wisdom, truth and understanding in a world of confusion and chaos.

I thank God that I have had the privilege of being Ronda's pastor.

Dr. Vince Gappa

BREATHE: THIS TOO SHALL PASS!

1 DETOUR AHEAD

"Give yourselves to God . . . surrender your whole being to Him to be used for righteous purposes." Romans 6:13 TEV

Mary and Joseph had plans for a nice, quiet life together then God changed it up. He chose her to be the mother of his son, Jesus. To Mary's question, "How can this be, since I am a virgin?" came the reply, "The Holy Spirit will come upon you, and the power of the Most High will overshadow you." Ready or not a new normal entered her life. Sometimes the road goes right when you want to go left.

Joseph, the son of Jacob, knew his father loved him. This was a fact that his eleven brothers deeply resented. God showed Joseph in a dream, that one day his brothers would bow down and pay homage to him.

What he did not see was the season of leadership-preparation on the horizon. He never expected the mandatory detour that would be required of him.

Beautiful Esther, an orphan, made her home with her cousin Mordecai. As his adopted daughter, he taught her well. The road turned decidedly to the right with the summons that sent her to the palace of the king. She appeared before him, and the King chose her as his next queen. I wonder, did she ever question her readiness for the responsibilities of royalty? From a common girl to the palace of a king! What an unexpected turn of events.

Are you there?

Your carefully laid plans have come to naught. You had hoped to go to college, but it did not work out. Someone you love is dying, or has died, and you feel isolated and afraid. You lost that baby you longed for through miscarriage, stillbirth, or early infant death. Dreams, so carefully nurtured in your heart, have never materialized through an accident, a poor choice, or lack of finances. You gave your heart to a suitor who proved to be untrue. The sting of rejection is fresh, and you agonize, searching for an answer to the question, "What went wrong?" Life feels empty. Tormented, you wonder how you are going to explain this turn of events to others.

You doubt if the dream God has given you will ever happen.

BREATHE: THIS TOO SHALL PASS!

Deep inside you search for an answer. You are drowning in the waters of your grief. "Why?" remains an unanswered question that nags at you into the wee hours of the morning. You are afraid, uneasy, deeply distressed. "Does Jesus care?" you whisper; and the dark night of your soul seems unending.

Prayer: "Help God. The bottom has fallen out of my life. Hear my cry for help. Open your ears and listen to my cry for mercy. My life is a prayer. I will wait to see what you will do. I will trust you. I will wait for morning when the sun shines again." Psalm 130 TEV

Breathe: This too shall pass. God has a plan.

2 PURPOSE IN THE PAIN

"The thought of my suffering . . . is bitter beyond words. I will never forget this awful time, as I grieve over my loss. Yet I still dare to hope when I remember this: The faithful love of the Lord never ends! His mercies never cease. Great is His faithfulness; His mercies begin afresh each morning. I say to myself. 'The Lord is my inheritance; therefore, I will hope in Him!' " Lamentations 3:19-24 NLT

What an honor to be the mother of the most high. An honor, yes, but not even Mary could foresee the turmoil that sacred event would bring to her life. In the immediate, how could she explain to her beloved Joseph, her family, her friends, the people of her town that she was going to have a baby?

One day, though she did not know it yet, she would weep in the shadow of the cross as her precious son died for the sins of humankind. What God asked of her was no small thing.

When Joseph was thrown into the pit, and later sold into slavery, did he question, "Why?" When he ran through the palace, after Potiphar's wife unsuccessfully tried to seduce him, was there terror in his heart as he heard her cries of "RAPE!" echoing through the halls? Were there moments as he sat, an innocent man in Potiphar's prison, when he wondered if the dream given to him years before was valid?

When Mordecai forbade Esther to reveal her nationality and family background to anyone (including her new husband) were there moments when she felt uneasy and troubled? When she learned that her people, the Jews, were to be annihilated, and that she was their only hope of salvation, was she afraid?

What did Mary, Joseph and Esther have in common? The plans and dreams they had so carefully made for their own lives did not happen. They had planned to go left, God said, "Go right."

Were there moments when they wondered, "Did I miss it somewhere? What is going on? Where is God?" They had not missed it, divine intervention planned a better path.

BREATHE: THIS TOO SHALL PASS!

The detour they were on was God-ordained. It was necessary and of great importance. God knew that in order for his plan to reach fulfillment, they had to be ready, and readiness for each of them, required a season of testing - intense testing.

Life has not gone as you planned. Switching directions was not your idea. Still, in obedience to his will, you took the road less traveled and now everything feels wrong. The night is black. The path unfamiliar. You are quite certain you are hopelessly lost.

Stop! God has not forgotten you.

Reach for him; he is there. Where you are right now is where you need to be. Yes, life hurts. It hurts for a reason. God is growing you up. He is preparing you. *"It is doubtful whether God can use a man greatly, until first He hurts him deeply,"* said A.W. Tozer.

You can rest in this: the darkness has not changed God's character. He still loves, he is still faithful, and he is still in control.

You do not understand and he may or may not give you an explanation. What he will give you, is himself. That my friend is enough. Just ask.

Prayer: "Father, I'm not particularly happy about the detour I have had to take in life. I need you to help me to rejoice when I run into problems and trials because, whether I like them or not, they are good for me. They help me to be patient. Patience develops strength of character in me and helps me to trust you more each time I use it until finally my hope and faith will be strong and steady. When that happens, I will be able to hold my head high no matter what happens and know that all is well, for I know how dearly you love me, and I will feel this warm love everywhere within me because you have given me the Holy Spirit to fill my heart with your love" (Based on Romans 5:3-5).

Breathe: This too shall pass. God has a plan.

3 PREPARATION

Pressing on when we do not understand, is part of the faith walk. Some turn away, disillusioned and disappointed when they don't understand the why. When life hurts, there is a truth that holds me steady. Suffering does play a key role.

God can bring good out of every instance of suffering and evil *if I let him*. If I put my trust in him, if I listen with an open and humble heart, and get out of his way.

It is not easy but it is necessary. It humbles me.

First in the list of reasons.

"And thou shalt remember all the way which the Lord thy God led thee, these forty years in the wilderness, to humble thee, and to prove thee, to know what was in thine heart . . . that he might make thee know that man doth not live by bread only, but by every word that proceedeth out of the mouth of the Lord . . ." Deuteronomy 8:2, 3 KJV

Suffering reminds me that he is more than enough for me. ". . . that is why, for Christ's sake, I delight in weaknesses, in insults, in hardships, in persecutions, in difficulties. For when I am weak, then I am strong." II Corinthians 12:10 NIV

It furthers his plan. ". . . I was physically broken, and so, prevented from continuing my journey, I was forced to stop with you. That is how I came to preach to you." Galatians 4:13 MSG

It reveals what is in my heart. "God withdrew from Hezekiah in order to test him and to see what was really in his heart." II Chronicles 32:31 NLT

It grows me up and teaches me truth. "Consider it a sheer gift, when tests and challenges come at you from all sides. You know that under pressure, your faith-life appears into the open and shows its true colors. So don't try to get out of anything prematurely. Let it do its work so you become mature and well developed, not deficient in any way. . . Anyone who meets a testing challenge head-on and manages to stick it out is fortunate. For such persons loyally in love with God, the reward is life and more life." James 1:2-8

BREATHE: THIS TOO SHALL PASS!

(MSG) reshapes us "In the same way, the Spirit helps us in our weakness . . . And we know that in all things God works for the good of those who love him, who have been called according to his purpose. For those God foreknew he also predestined to be conformed to the likeness of his Son . . ." Romans 8:26-29 NIV

It shifts my focus heavenward. "Blessed is the man who perseveres under trial, because when he has stood the test, he will receive the crown of life that God has promised to those who love him." James 1:12 NIV

For Mary, even death could not win in the darkest night of her soul. Her dead son lay in a sepulcher of stone, but three days later, her weeping turned to joy when Jesus walked out of that tomb. Mary chose to be faithful to her son and faithful to her God. She invested her life in Jesus, and through him, came the greatest gift the world has ever known: salvation.

Joseph, the son of Jacob, chose to see the handiwork of God in the circumstances of his life. Out of the dark night of his soul, emerged one of the greatest examples of forgiveness in scripture. To his weeping, bowing brothers he spoke "You meant it for evil, but God meant it for good."

Esther chose to believe that God had a purpose and a plan even in the midst of the darkest night of her life. She found courage to do the seeming impossible, and in doing so gave us one of the greatest example of courage in scripture. She showed us that sometimes God allows us to pass through the most difficult of times to fashion us into his image, to bring us to just this time, at just this moment, to touch our world for him.

Author Max Lucado says it well, "God sees our life from beginning to end. He may lead us through a storm at age thirty so we can endure a hurricane at age sixty . . . Should God place you on his anvil, be thankful. It means he thinks you're still worth reshaping."

Prayer: "I will walk by faith even when I cannot see because this broken road prepares your will for me. Amen" (Jeremy Camp).

Breathe: This too shall pass. God has a plan.

4 THROUGH IT ALL

"Acquaint now thyself with him, and be at peace . . ." Job 22:21

I was young, and over 1700 miles away from home. Most of the time, I was alone. A military man, my husband was often away for weeks at a time. I kept busy mothering my two children, actively participating in a weekly women's Bible study, and occasionally stepping out of my comfort zone to tickle the ivories for morning worship at the church where we attended.

On those mornings, more often than not, my young son Paul sat on a chair directly behind the piano. It was a compromise of sorts. What he really wanted was to be on the bench with me, but he could not keep his toddler fingers off the keyboard. Diana, my youngest, was a babe in arms and I never lacked for willing arms to hold her while I played.

This particular morning, I was not at the piano, I was standing in front of the congregation, microphone in hand, singing my vow to God. "I'll do anything to be closer to you." Growing up, life had been idyllic. Since launching into adulthood, it had been anything but. I had lived long enough to know that sometimes life is hard and lonely. The lyrics flowing from my lips were heartfelt and sincere. I loved God and I wanted to follow him wherever he led me.

I had no idea that morning where my commitment would take me in the years to come. The future stretched before me full of possibilities. I imagined chapter titles that were 'short and sweet': Sunshine, Gentle Breezes, Sweet Platitudes, and Tranquility. Whatever came my way, I was determined to walk it with Jesus. I loved him; he loved me – we would do this together.

The chapter titles changed though, reflecting the dark side of life - Poor Choices, Broken Dreams, Assault, Relinquishment, Abandonment, and Abuse. It has been forty years since that memorable Sunday morning. I have changed.

I am who I am today because of the difficult times. God knew exactly where he would take me and he prepared me to go there. What has not changed is my commitment to him. I am still walking the walk with Jesus.

BREATHE: THIS TOO SHALL PASS!

The final pages of my story are being written. All too soon my journey will be complete. Without hesitation, I thank God for the storms he has brought me through safely. Now I know that God can calm them, I know what faith in him can do. I still do not like pain, but I see it differently today. It is a tool that God can use to shape and control my life. Through it all, I've learned to trust in Jesus.

How do you look at pain? As a tool to fashion your life, or a weapon to batter and break you? God has the pain under control.

Prayer: "Father, if this problem, pain, sickness, or circumstance is needed to fulfill your purpose and glory in my life, or in another's, please don't take it away." (Rick Warren)

Breathe: This too shall pass. God has a plan.

BREATHE: THIS TOO SHALL PASS!

5 THAT'S WHAT GRACE IS FOR

" ... My grace is sufficient for thee: for my strength is made perfect in weakness." II Corinthians 12:9

Though the waiting area next to the Radiation-Oncology department at St. Joseph Hospital is spacious, I feel like I am suffocating. We make our way to a wooden bench next to a gently flowing waterfall, and make small talk. "I heard them read the twenty-third Psalm over the PA system a little while ago," she says, "they said today might be a hard day."

A wheelchair across the way cradles a tiny woman in its cold, unmoving arms. Angry burns from radiation wrap like a necklace around her reddened neck. I'm sure she would rather be on a cruise basking in the warm, soothing rays of the Caribbean sun.

Instead, she faces rays of another kind - blistering, unmerciful, and unwelcome. "Faithful are the wounds of a friend," scripture says. Some friend this radiation. She has no choice but to walk arm in arm with her. Anything less will cost her life.

Through the window, I see another woman walking. Tall and stately, but obviously ill. A turban covers her balding head. Her floral print dress hangs loosely on her body and I wonder if her foe is breast cancer. I wonder, too, what tomorrow holds for her.

We settle onto a bench just outside of radiology, a cup of hot chocolate cradled in our hands. Neither of us really wants it, we just hope that it will warm our tummies, and soothe our battered souls.

She starts to speak, then stops and begins to cry. "I can't believe we're here. Why can't God just take us when he's ready, instead of letting us suffer?"

I immediately think of all kinds of theological sounding things to say. You know, things like, "Suffering makes us strong. It sensitizes us to a hurting world, equips us for ministry, fashions us into the image of Jesus Christ. Why, I'm learning that there is added purpose in our suffering when it gives courage to others in their grief." It would make a great outline for a five-part sermon, but today it lacks punch. God seems to whisper in my ear, "Put your lips together and hush. She doesn't need a sermon, she needs a shoulder."

BREATHE: THIS TOO SHALL PASS!

It is sad. To another person, on another day, I might actually have said those words, but, this is not just another person, this is my Momma and, it isn't just another day. This is the day my Daddy becomes an unwitting contender in the battle for his life.

We cry together, and then sit quietly for a while. "It would be ok," she says, "if you just woke up one morning, and God said, 'this is the day,' and then he just took you home."

"Yes," I say, "You could get up, make your bed, brush your teeth, and then just go."

"You wouldn't have to brush your teeth," she muses.

"Or, make your bed for that matter," I quip. We share a smile, and then we do the difficult thing; we just sit and wait, each of us lost in thought. I have been dreading this day since Saturday when Mom called to let me know that Dad would have his first appointment with radiology this morning. She only hinted, but was measurably relieved when I said, "Do you want me to be there?"

This is all new to me. We have had lots of cancer in our family, but it has never been my dad's cancer before. Yesterday I sat in the parking lot near a small lake south of town and cried. Broken, and confused, my head throbbing and my stomach churning.

"I . . . don't . . . want . . . my. . . Daddy . . . to . . . die," I sobbed over the cell phone to my husband Rob.

The sun was setting when I pointed the car toward home. Turning the corner into our neighborhood, I was suddenly aware that I could not even remember making the drive. Dad and Mom have always been my tower of strength, now I must be theirs. "Father, please help me," I prayed, "I need to be there for them tomorrow and I don't have anything to give."

When God speaks, his words speak life. Early this morning he whispered one simple phrase to my heart, "That's what grace is for."

Sitting beside my weeping mom, and drying tears of my own, I feel so helpless. I wish for words to make it go away. I wish I were a little girl again. I wish she were scolding me for an unmade bed, or a messy sink. I want her to smile, I want her to laugh, and I can't make it so. God gently reminds me, "It's ok that you don't know what to say. I know they are the dearest on earth to you. Trust me with her hurting heart. Trust me with his broken body. Let me care for them. That's what grace is for."

I feel so small, and weak, and very much alone. He reminds me that life is tough. "I know it's hard. I know you feel fragile. I will be your strength. Let me carry you. That's what grace is for."

"This was really hard to do today," Mom says as she hands me the legal document that gives permission to the doctors to remove life support from my dad should we reach that point.

I feel my heart wrench. I do not want to read this. I see dad's initials confirming his wishes, and pray that day will never come. Tomorrow is uncertain; the future seems so bleak. God whispers, "Don't fear tomorrow for I am already there." In a few days, we will do this all over again, and when we do, he will be present, as he is today.

I rest in the knowing that they are his, and he will never leave them. In the dark of their night, he will sit beside them, and he will sing to them. I am tired, but my heart is at peace. I snuggle into the Father's arms and he holds me. That's as it should be, that's what grace is for.

Breathe: This too shall pass. God has a plan.

6 'TIS SO SWEET

Even when I do not understand!

The muscles in my body cry out for relief from the top of my head to the tip of my toes. I hurt in places I didn't know could hurt. The hot pad and *Aleve* offered minimal relief. My husband Rob prayed for me, as he always does when the pain is bigger than I am. This is not how life is supposed to be, or is it?

God's been speaking to me about idols, to trust and surrender.

I *prefer* that my current life-song be, "I'm living on the mountain underneath the cloudless sky", or "If it keeps getting better and better, Oh Lord, I don't know what I'm gonna do". I *prefer* those songs because they speak of victory, soft breezes, sanctuary, and a safe place in the cleft of the rock.

Instead, my life-song has been, "Tis So Sweet to Trust in Jesus," a song that infers need and desperation, or else why would I need to trust? That was the only song I could think of, when I made the drive, back to my home, in Denver. Earlier that morning as I prepared to go to court, I was certain God had spoken to my heart, "If you look for me, I'll be there." I was *sure* that meant the one I loved so fiercely would be returning with me when the hearing was over. Instead, they arrested him on the spot.

Reeling with shock and keenly disappointed, I slammed my hand against the steering wheel and vented at God. "I thought you said you would be there! Where were *you*?" I cried my tears - buckets of them - but in the end the only song that brought me comfort was, "Tis So Sweet to Trust in Jesus." and that is what I sang.

I sang it a few months ago when my tiny granddaughter was oh so sick, and we wanted her to be well again. I sang it with the realization that fibromyalgia intended to stay, my new best friend, like it or not. I sang it again, when the bottom fell out of the auto market, and my husband's job of 23 years abruptly ended. I sang it when the bank account was empty. I sang it when the cupboards were bare. It was my song when we prayed for healing; but instead mourned, when the one I loved so much was laid to rest. I rested in it, one night not long ago, when in the stillness of the church sanctuary, I wept and brokenly whispered to God, "Is it okay if I just sit in your presence because I can't think of anything to say?" I have sung it, and sung it and sung it again, and in the singing, I came to embrace the truth.

I said God has been teaching me three things, now I remember one more. God is teaching me the importance of submitting to brokenness. It is a scary place to be even when you know the breaking is for a purpose. I am still learning, but I am closer than I was before. I know with certainty that I can walk hand-in-hand with brokenness, because I know it gloves the hand of my Savior. Because it does, I can trust even when I don't understand.

Instead of resisting, submit to the breaking He is allowing in your life. It isn't pleasant; it isn't fun, but I can tell you without hesitation, there *is* purpose or he would not allow it. You can trust the One who went to Calvary for you. You can trust him as he works *himself* into your life. Rest in what you know to be true about him. Don't despair. You will get through this to the other side if you trust him. 'Tis so sweet to trust in Jesus . . . oh for grace to trust him more.

Breathe: This too shall pass. God has a plan.

7 ON THE EDGE

Word on the street is that there is a spectacular view from this vantage point. I wouldn't know having never been here before. Tonight this Rocky Mount is shrouded in darkness, the eerie calm broken only by my chattering teeth and knocking knees.

Frankly, just between us, I do not like this kind of adventure. If God hadn't called, I wouldn't be here. I would be home in front of the fire, basking in the warmth of my comfort zone. Instead, I am out in the cold, alone, teetering on the brink of an abyss. My only consolation comes in knowing that it can't get any worse. Then it does. With terrifying brilliance, lightning explodes on the horizon, thunder splinters the stillness, and heaven dumps buckets of freezing rain right where I am standing. My tears mingle with the driving mizzle, dripping off my chin.

Above the din, I think I hear a voice calling my name. For a fleeting moment, another burst of lightning chases the darkness away. There, at the bottom of my crag, I see a man. He waves, and then with hands cupped about his mouth, he calls my name once more.

I know that voice. It is Jesus. Lord of Lords, King of Kings, Lover of my Soul, the one who called me out into the storm. In another place, at another time, I would bow down and call him Holy. Now, cold and hungry, weakened by the fury of the storm, I am angry. *What does he want? Why did he call me out only to leave me alone? This is how he treats his own?*

He knows I am wrestling with my emotions. He knows, because I am his, and he knows me through and through. A gust of wind sticks its finger in my back, and pushes me closer to the edge. My anger changes to terror. Without him, I will perish. *Lord, help me! Tell me what to do!*

"Jump!"

"Jump! Excuse me. I don't think I heard you right. What did you say?"

"Jump, I'll catch you!"

Surely, He jests. His request evokes memories of other times, in other places when someone said, "Jump!" and I did. Only they did not catch me, they walked away, and I hit the ground.

BREATHE: THIS TOO SHALL PASS!

Me jump? Why should I trust him any more than I trust those others?

Because while I hid my pain on a shelf in the closet of my heart, God loved me. He held me, and, when the time was right, we opened the door together, unwrapped the package, and exposed it to his light.

How can I *not* trust him? I may not understand. I may not even like where he takes me. This I do know: he will never leave me to suffer alone. When my heart shatters, he will put it together, making it stronger than before. In the night hours, when I weep, he will sit by my bed and sing to me. He will redeem my pain; make me a planting for himself that he might be glorified. He will turn my darkness into light. For my ashes, give me beauty. At the edge, when there is nowhere else to go, he will provide a way out.

Jesus. Lord of Lords. King of Kings. Lover of my Soul. Catch me. I'm jumping.

Breathe: This too shall pass. God has a plan.

8 TOUCHING GOD FOR MY OWN

They are called sacred moments. Those unexpected pauses in time, when the divine interrupts the human, and you throw back your head and laugh aloud in wonder. I had one of those moments the other day.

"Pour out your heart like water before the face of the Lord ... Lift up your hands toward him for the lives of your children." Lamentations 2:19

The tank was full, and I was going home. Home to dad and mom. Home to their arms. Home to their reassurances that I am loved. Home to a love that says, "You're not a failure." More importantly, I was going home to their reminders of the faithfulness of the God we love, to ride out the darkest storms with us.

RONDA KNUTH

I am a grandma myself, but age does not matter when you are talking about the unconditional love of godly parents. It is the same at fifty as it was at five. I have a burden for my prodigal.

It is an ache of its own, this knowing that the child you birthed, battles emotionally naked, defenseless against the forces of evil. It is a helpless feeling- and the desire to "make it all o.k.", wrestles with the wisdom of knowing that this precious man-child of mine, must reach the end of himself before he will bow to God. He will have to face the consequences of his choices.

Once God said of Paul the apostle, in scripture, "It is hard for you to kick against the pricks." It is hard for my son, too.

On my way to the restaurant where my adult son and I had agreed to meet I prayed, "God, this is the scariest thing I've ever done. My words may cause anger, and this one I love might walk out of my life forever . . . but it's a risk I'm willing to take."

He slipped into the booth a wary look on his face. "I want to know what's going on, son." I could see in his eyes the mental mêlée taking place. *How much do I tell her? What does she already know?*

He spilled, and I countered, "If you were two years old, I'd know how to handle this." He is not two years old- he's a grown man now. I calmly expressed my concerns, and then instead of scolding I clasped his hands in mine and whispered, "I adore you, my son. You are mine. I love you, and nothing you do will ever change that love. God has given me a promise concerning you son, and I'm not giving up."

The miles slipped by as I remembered those hours. I fumbled through my box of comfort music, and slipped one into the player. First one tear and then another traced its way down my cheek as the words settled over my heart. The words of the song spoke of the greatness of my God and his ability to make a way when there doesn't appear to be one. Just a few years before I'd found comfort on this same road when, in a raging rain storm, I'd heard the words of another song tenderly encouraging a weary mom not to give up hope – her son, her daughter is reachable.

There had not been much progress since then, but I still struggled to believe. Isn't that what faith is all about- believing in the face of the impossible? As my thoughts turned heavenward, I found myself interceding for my son- first with words that were measured, and contained; then with tortured sobs. "Lord, save my son. Show him your glory. Turn his heart to you and do it in such a way, that he will know that it is you who is turning his heart."

One mile, ten, thirty and still I pressed in knowing that this weary mother was having audience with Almighty God. I wept silent tears; I pled at the top of my voice; I agonized in the depths of my soul. Then it happened! Scripture describes it as a *peace that passes understanding.* It did not make sense. Nothing had changed, but the burden lifted, and I had peace in that moment. A tiny bubble of joy made its way from deep inside me, and exploded in praise from my lips. I laughed aloud in wonder, shedding tears of a different sort- cleansing, healing tears of praise. "Oh, my God," I cried, "You are holy. You are majestic. You are faithful. You can do anything. I believe should this be."

I think God laughed with me, "Ahh, she's getting it." Then I think he cried.

I rounded the corner, tear-weary, and pulled into the driveway. Through that door were my dad and mom. I still wanted to feel their arms, to hear their reassurances, to revel in their love. I needed them just because of who they are - not because of what they could give me. I had come in search of peace, but had already found it, somewhere out there on Interstate 76.

Outwardly, nothing changed, but I believe. I believe that God, who fashioned my son in his own image, knows exactly how to draw him near to himself. I believe that even when I cannot see God working, he is. I believe that I can trust him with this one, who means so much to me. I believe that the effectual, fervent prayer of a righteous mom availeth much. I believe that God will turn the world upside down to turn the heart of my son to himself. I watch. I wait. I pray. I believe.

Breathe: This too shall pass. God has a plan.

9 LORD, I WANT TO BE REAL

If being real means I am alone, and in that solitude you walk with me, then let me be alone, led in the moment only by you.

If being real means that I struggle with the weakness of others, and wonder at my ability to handle a difficult situation, but in that awareness you join me on my journey, quickening my heart, and sharpening my senses, then let me struggle . . . let me wonder . . . let me be aware.

If being real means that I grapple with where I am in the world, but in my wrestling, you stand by me, call my name, and bear me in your everlasting arms; then let me continue wrestling. Hold me in such a way, that I cannot loosen your grip.

Lord, I want to be real. If being real means that I question and there are no answers, but in my questioning I learn to trust your Word, your character, your love, then let me question, let me listen only to your voice.

If being real means that I am confused, not knowing which way to go- that I struggle with sadness and wonder why you are silent - but in that bewilderment you walk with me, then let me be unsure; let me seek your face, clinging tightly to your hand.

If being real means that I am exhausted to the core, but in my weariness, you sit by my bed, and sing to me, your fingers entwine with mine, and you gently whisper my name, then I will be weary resting in your tender care.

If being real means that I hurt, or walk with another who is hurting, and in that time of intense emotion you are there soothing, teaching, lovingly speaking, "You are my own," then I will walk on for you, my hand safely tucked in yours.

Lord, I want to be real. If being real means that my body must ache, and sometimes I forget to smile through the tears, but in my pain, you become my strength, my comfort, my joy; then I will ache on, safe in the shelter of your embrace. Not because I welcome suffering with open arms, but because I welcome you. More importantly, you welcome me.

BREATHE: THIS TOO SHALL PASS!

When I am faithless, you remain faithful. God of my life let me lean on you.

Fold me closely to your bosom; bathe me with your presence. Not just my hands and feet, Lord, but all of me, *wash all of me, with you.*

Let the light of your countenance shine on me. Search me, O God and know my heart. As I journey through the process, teach me what it means to rest in your sovereignty.

Breathe: This too shall pass. God has a plan.

10 A SONG IN THE NIGHT

During the day, she kept busy going to appointments, playing games on her computer, and helping to manage the properties she and my dad owned in eastern Colorado. At night, when the rest of the world was sleeping, she had time to think. She worried about treatments – which were good, which were not? She was sad knowing that unless God intervened on her behalf, she was going to die. She and dad had been together since they were teens. What would happen to him? She was sad when she thought about leaving her family, often saying, "Maybe I love them too much."

Mom fought long and hard. Many days she suffered indescribable pain. Only near the end did she take to her bed. When she could no longer get out of bed, the hospice nurse suggested a monitor.

One beside mom's bed and one in the living room next to my dad's chair so he could hear if she needed him. One night I sat in the living room with dad. We shut the door to the bedroom, hoping that mom would rest. A few minutes passed and then, over the monitor, we heard singing. Mom's voice cracked with age and weariness, but it was beautiful:

"Jesus, Jesus, Jesus, there's just something about that name. Master, Saviour, Jesus . . ." the sleep medication blurred her words. She finished the refrain and then there was a brief moment of silence before she launched into another song. The tears rolled silently down my cheeks.

Mom started singing herself to sleep a couple of years before she died. She sang songs about heaven, songs of longing for Jesus, songs of trust and songs of surrender. One night I laid on the bed next to her in the darkness, her hand tucked in mine. She started singing, then stopped and invited, "Sing with me. I sing," she said between songs, "So God won't forget where I am."

"Oh, mama," I sobbed, "God will never forget you."

"Do you think heaven is real?" she asked. I suppose when you are so close to eternity you question many things. Do I? I wondered. I hesitated for only a moment before saying, "Yes, mama; I know that heaven is real."

It is that assurance that gives me the courage to face a tomorrow without her. Mom sang as an expression of her faith in the dark night of her soul. She sang *just because*, it is what she did when life came crashing down.

I looked at dad, settled comfortably in his recliner. He, too, was weeping. For one "sweet beyond words" moment, I forgot that mother was dying. My spirit calmed. I was a little girl again listening to her sing. I felt safe and loved. God had not forgotten mother. Life was crashing down, and he was there with a beautiful song in the night.

Breathe: This too shall pass. God has a plan.

11 MORE THAN I CAN BEAR

"Calling the crowd to join His disciples, He said, 'anyone who intends to come with me has to let me lead. You're not in the driver's seat; I am. Don't run from suffering; embrace it. Follow me and I'll show you how. Self-help is no help at all. Self-sacrifice is the way, my way, to saving yourself, your true self. What good would it do to get everything you want and lose you, the real you? What could you ever trade your soul for?' " Mark 8:34-38 MSG

What they said about God not allowing you to go through more than you can bear . . . it isn't true. That is what I was told when I buried my son, when my marriage dissolved, when I was assaulted, when my best-friend-mom suffered, then died. I wondered then if it was true - it sure felt like more than I could bear. When abandoned, defamed, misunderstood, and rejected, I wondered if it were true. If it were, God thought me stronger than I thought me to be.

I wanted to give up. I did not feel strong. I knew I couldn't make it; it wasn't in me to survive.

But God! He made the difference. He made it possible for me to go through what I could not bear. I came to the end of myself and I ran to him. He embraced me. He loved me. He gave me the strength to face the unthinkable. That is not a bad place to be.

In the beginning, it was an uncomfortable place to be. I was used to "doing life" in my own power. Leaning on him assumed that I trust him, and I was not sure if I did. If he would allow this level of sorrow in my life, could I trust Him?

I was not doing a very good job on my own so I made a choice to trust him. It was the least I could do for the one who went to Calvary for me. If good could come of my pain, it would be because my Redeemer God would bring that good out of the bad.

T.D. Jakes sums it up this way

"God says, "I need some people who have gone through the fire and have not been destroyed or burned up by it as a sign that God's gonna get some glory out of it. Sometimes God has to let your troubles 'get outside' so everyone sees it. They say, 'He's down and can't get up.' Then comes Jesus. When others see you go through something that should have destroyed you and you're saying, 'He stayed with me. I will trust Him!' What a testimony. I need some people who have gone through it and come out on the other side so they can say, 'God was able, and God was faithful. He'll be with you as He was with me.' There are manifestations

of God's presence that you will only know by being tested. There are some things you learn about Him only in the fire. God wants to use your situation to teach others you don't even know, about how to go through troubles. God knows He can trust you to go through this, and to come out on the other side with a testimony of triumph on your lips."

He is worth trusting. I have found him to be a faithful friend.

Prayer: "I want to know you, Lord. To really know you. Do in me all that you need to do that you might do through me all that you long to do."

Breathe: This too shall pass. God has a plan.

12 THE MASTER PLAN

"This is the kind of life you've been invited into, the kind of life Christ lived. He suffered everything that came his way so you would know that it could be done, and also know how to do it, step-by-step." I Peter 2:21 MSG

God is God; I am not. I answer to Him, not he to me. Because that is so, he doesn't have to explain why he allows suffering in my life. He does give us a number of general reasons in his Word.

When I suffer: My sensitivity to a hurting world increases. "Praise be to the God and Father of our Lord Jesus Christ, the Father of compassion and the God of all comfort, who comforts us in all our troubles, so that we can comfort those in any trouble with the comfort we ourselves have received from God." II Corinthians 1:3-4 NIV

Others find courage in their own suffering.

"I want to report to you, friends, that my imprisonment here has had the opposite of its intended effect. Instead of being squelched, the Message has actually prospered. All the soldiers here, and everyone else too, found out that I'm in jail because of the Messiah. That piqued their curiosity, and now they've learned all about Him. Not only that, but most of the Christians here have become far more sure of themselves in the faith than ever than ever, speaking out fearlessly about God, about the Messiah . . . I can hardly wait to continue on my course. I don't expect to be embarrassed in the least. On the contrary, everything happening to me in jail only serves to make Christ more accurately known, regardless of whether I live or die. They didn't shut me up; they gave me a pulpit!" Philippians 1:12-14; 20 MSG

My desires are clarified and prioritized. *"Think of your sufferings as a weaning from that old sinful habit of always expecting to get your own way. Then you'll be able to live out your days free to pursue what God wants instead of being tyrannized by what you want."* I Peter 4: 1-2 MSG

I am purified: *"Pure gold put in the fire comes out of it proved pure; genuine faith put through this suffering comes out proved genuine. When Jesus wraps this all up, it's your faith, not your gold that God will have on display as evidence of his victory."* I Peter 1:7 MSG

"Friends, when life gets really difficult, don't jump to the conclusion that God isn't on the job. Instead, be glad that you are in the very thick of what Christ experienced. This is a spiritual refining process, with glory just around the corner." I Peter 4:12-13 MSG

BREATHE: THIS TOO SHALL PASS!

I learn the true meaning of worship. *"Though the fig tree does not bud and there are no grapes on the vines, though the olive crop fails and the fields produce no food, though there are no sheep in the pen and no cattle in the stalls, yet, I will rejoice in the Lord, I will be joyful in God my Savior."* Habakkuk 3:17-18 NIV

". . . Give thanks in all circumstances, for this is God's will for you in Christ Jesus." I Thessalonians 5:18 NIV

"Through Him, therefore, let us constantly and at all times offer up to God a sacrifice of praise, which is the fruit of lips that thankfully acknowledge and confess and glorify His name." Hebrews 13:15 AMP

"Worshippers are not made during the good times. Worshippers are made in the fires of affliction- during the dark stormy nights when you don't have an answer for what you are going through. They are made during the lonely times – when you don't know for sure (except for God) how anything is going to work out. How you respond during these times, how you deal with the fiery storms of life will determine the kind of worshipper you become. . ." - George Morrison.

Prayer: "Lord, teach me to dance and to praise you in the tough times. I want to learn to worship you in spirit and in truth." John 4:24

Breathe: This too shall pass. God has a plan.

13 DESERT JOURNEY

Nothing is right. It is hotter than hades. It's dry and I'm covered in a haze of dust. My feet hurt, my throat is parched, and I silently curse the blistering sun. I did not sign up for this. Despair hangs like an albatross around my neck. I would give all I own, and then some, for a shady tree, and a cup of cold water. *How much longer God?*

The incline is not steep, but it feels insurmountable. A few more steps and I will be at the top. Hope sticks a finger in my back and pushes me on. Maybe there is an oasis on the other side. Sweet water, soft grass, shade beneath a palm. I will drink my fill, and then I will rest. Maybe I will just stay there forever. I can do this. Just a little farther. I crest the hill and scan the horizon. Nothing. There is nothing but more sand and sun. Where is God? Doesn't he care? I would weep but why bother? I am alone. Utterly alone.

A dot in the distance catches my eye. *Is someone coming my way?* Just as quickly, I douse my hope. It is better not to believe. I bow my head and stagger on. "You are God" I challenge, not even sure he is listening. "You could get me out of here if you wanted. I am here; you are not. You don't care!"

If I stop, I die. I plod on – one hour, three, then five. I am so tired. I forget about the dot in the distance until I round the bend. I rub my eyes, certain that the man with a wagon pulled by a mule is nothing more than a figment of my imagination. The donkey brays, the man speaks, and exhausted, I sprawl in the dirt at his feet, "Please sir, I beg you. Please help me!"

Unable to move, totally at his mercy, I wait. My life is in his hands. What will he do? I hope that he is kind. He bends low and pulls me into his arms. They are strong; they are tender, like a momma with her newborn baby. I lay my head against his breast and hear the beating of his heart. He turns and carefully lays me in the bed of the wagon under the shade of his tarp. No more dry dust, no more simmering sun. He slips my shoes from my blistered swollen feet. Eyes closed, I surrender to his care.

I feel rather than see as he presses the lip of his canteen against my mouth. "Just a sip, maybe two. There you go. There is plenty more where that came from." He moistens a kerchief from his pocket and carefully soothes as he washes my hot, red face. Tears of gratitude and relief mingle with the water wiping away the grime. With cool water in a basin, he bathes my fingers then my feet.

BREATHE: THIS TOO SHALL PASS!

"Rest now," he whispers brushing the hair from my brow, "I will care for you." A soft pillow cradles my head; a clean sheet is my cover. Utterly spent, I sleep in the shadow of His hand.

When I waken, the moon has replaced the sun in the sky. A cool breeze tickles my face. *Am I dreaming?* The scent of supper wafts my way. My stomach rumbles. I cannot remember the last time I ate. Whoever this stranger is, he is God's gift to me. I stretch, slip from the wagon, and walk toward the fire.

"Hello!" I hear a smile in his words. He rises, sets aside his own dish, then turns to ladle a generous portion of porridge into a bowl. "You must be hungry!" He calls me by name and I like the sound of it on his lips. *I do not remember telling him who I am.*

"Sit down, eat. Would you like something cold to drink?"

Thank you. Thank you so much! I eat and drink until I am satisfied. That is when I look at him – really look at him - for the first time. There is something about him . . . *Jesus? Jesus, is it you?*

"It is. You prayed. I came."

"What took you so long?"

He laughs, I smile, and then we talk heart-to-heart. I tell him about my journey. Nobody asked me if I wanted to go, life just demanded it. I knew it would be hard, not this hard, but I'm not complaining Lord. He looks at me. Okay; yes I am! Then I get real with him. I thought you forgot me.

In a torrent of words, I spill all the hurt, the doubt, the anger, and the disappointment. He does not answer right away, or dismiss what I have said with platitudes. I am glad he knows. I know that it has been bad. I use up all my words then we just sit together listening to the crackle of the fire. It is enough – for now –just to be in his presence.

"I'm not tired," he finally says. "I will keep watch. Why don't you get some sleep?"

I crawl back into the wagon and settle in for the night. My thirst quenched, my stomach full, I close my eyes and listen to his voice in the darkness. He's singing, a song, for me.

"Jesus?"

"I'm here."

Wake me when you are ready. I cannot wait to get out of this desolate place.

He may have answered, I do not know if he did. I closed my eyes, and slept the sleep of the blessed.

Maybe it is the warmth of the sun, or the rolling of the wheels on the road. Whatever it is I wake with a start. I stretch, toss back the tarp, and climb next to him on the seat. I know I am welcome.

"Good morning! Feel better?"

"Much, thank you for letting me sleep." I smile; he smiles. We push on in companionable silence.

BREATHE: THIS TOO SHALL PASS!

It is early afternoon before I realize . . . wait a minute, we are going the wrong way! We are going deeper into the desert.

"You have to my child. The only way to the other side is by going through."

My face crumples then I give way to gut-wrenching sobs. *I trusted him. How could he? I* don't like this place. Why can't we leave? Why do we have to be here?

He takes my hand in his, pulls on the reins, slows the mule and stops the wagon.

"Please, Lord. Please don't make me do this. It's too hard. I'm tired. I want to go home. My body hurts, my heart is sick, my faith is gone."

"Going back is not an option." His words are firm, fused with love. "Pressing on, in my name, is what we do when life is hard. You are not alone. We will do this together."

The road is still dusty, and the sun is still hot. We are not "there" yet, wherever "there" might be. It is okay, I am going to make it. He knows where we are going; he has been this way before. He quiets me with his love. Everything is going to be all right.

"Casting all your care upon him for he careth for you." I Peter 5:7

Breathe: This too shall pass. God has a plan.

14 I AM HIS

"In my distress I called to the Lord; I cried to my God for help. From his temple he heard my voice; my cry came before him, into his ears." Psalm 18:6

It is business as usual in the courts of Heaven. Melodious songs of adoration fill the air, exalting the ever-faithful Lover of the universe. "Hosanna, Hosanna, Hosanna! Blessing, and glory, and wisdom, and thanksgiving, and honor, and power, and might be unto God for ever and ever."

Messengers, intent upon their assignments scurry, eager to do the Father's business. Constant motion; blessed peace. A smile, glorious, wondrous, and warm radiates from the Father's face, and he whispers, "This is good, very, very good." Then just as quickly, the smile is gone. Heaven senses the urgency of the moment, and stills. All eyes are upon the Father as he leans intently forward, and with quiet authority speaks: "Listen, my daughter is crying."

He bends his ear, intent upon my cry. He knows me. He loves me. I am his own. Yes, I am in trouble. The cords of death entangle me; the torrents of destruction overwhelm me. In my distress, I call to him for the Lord is my rock, my fortress, my deliverer. He is my refuge, my shield, my strength.

At once, before I finish my plea, he leaps into action. The earth trembles and quakes. The foundations of the mountains shake and tremble. My God, my rock, my strength- the very God of the universe is angry.

Smoke rises from his nostrils; a consuming fire, and blazing coals, come from his mouth. With a sudden fierceness, he parts the heavens, and *he comes down*. Dark clouds are under his feet. He mounts the cherubim, and begins to fly. He soars on the wings of the wind.

Darkness is his covering; the canopy about him, the dark rain clouds of the sky. Out of the brightness of his presence, clouds advance, with hailstones and bolts of lightning. I feel so alone. The storm frightens me. *I do not know that he is in the storm.*

Suddenly my Lord thunders from heaven; his voice- the voice of the Most High- the voice of my Father- reverberates through the darkness. He shoots his arrows, and my enemies scatter. With great bolts of lightning, he throws them into great tumult. At his rebuke, at the blast of breath from his nostrils, the valleys of the sea are exposed, and the foundations of the earth appear.

BREATHE: THIS TOO SHALL PASS!

Then he reaches down for me. He rescues me from my powerful enemy, from my foes who are too strong for me. My enemy, brazen and bold, confronts me in the day of my disaster, but the Lord is my support. He brought me out into a spacious place; he rescued me because he delights in me. Did you hear that? *The God of the universe, moved heaven and earth for me today, because he delights in me.*

You, O Lord, will keep my lamp burning; you my God will turn my darkness into light. With your help, I can advance against a troop; with you, I can scale a wall. It is God, who arms me with strength and makes my way perfect. He stoops down to make me great. *He arms me with strength for the battle.*

Though I am broken I will say, "The Lord lives! Praise be to my Rock! Exalted be God my Savior! I will praise you among the nations, O Lord; I will sing praises to your name. I am your anointed, and you show kindness to me."

He makes my enemies to bow at my feet. He makes them turn their backs in flight, and I will destroy them. The enemy cries for help, even to the Lord, but he does not answer them. They do not know him. They are not his own.

He knows me. He loves me. I am his own. "Listen, my daughter is crying." In praise and adoration to my King. Based on Psalm 18

Breathe: This too shall pass; God has a plan.

15 UNDER CONSTRUCTION

"We went through fire and water; but you brought us out to fulfillment." Psalm 66:12 TLB

It was the one night of the week, when you could find us all tightly scrunched together. We were sitting on the couch in front of the television, waiting to see the result. We watched the screen to see which deserving family they chose. While they went on an all-expense paid vacation, their home underwent an extreme transformation.

Sometimes the old was demolished, and a new house built from scratch. A whole team of designers, contractors and hundreds of other workers would descend on a site and in just seven days, a beautiful, take-your-breath-away abode emerged. The returning family was often overwhelmed with happiness when they saw their new house for the first time. So were we.

Invariably one of us would swipe at a tear, or let out a cheer as the episode unfolded. A lot of planning, measuring, sawing, hammering, blood, sweat and tears went into construction.

I too am a work in progress. God is not through with me yet. He is doing an extreme makeover of my life. He holds the master blueprint and a lot of planning, measuring, sawing, hammering, blood, sweat and tears is going into my renovation. One tool he uses as he restores my life is that of suffering. His work is purposeful. He does not bludgeon, he molds me with care fashioning me into the image of Christ. He also uses suffering to:

Draw me closer to His heart.

"The Lord is close to the brokenhearted; he rescues those who are crushed in spirit." Psalm 34:18 NLT

Teach me obedience.

"During the days of Jesus' life on earth, he offered up prayers and petitions with loud cries and tears to the one who could save him from death, and he was heard because of his reverent submission. Although he was a son, he learned obedience from what he suffered. . ." Hebrews 5:7-8 NIV

Bring me back to God when I am disobedient.
"And have you completely forgotten this word of encouragement that addresses you as a father addresses

his son? It says, 'My son, do not make light of the Lord's discipline, and do not lose heart when He rebukes you, because the Lord disciplines the one He loves, and He chastens everyone He accepts as His son. Endure hardship as discipline; God is treating you as His children. For what children are not disciplined by their father? . . . *All discipline for the moment seems not to be joyful but sorrowful, yet to those who have been trained by it.*" Hebrews 12:5-7, 11 NIV

Make Christ accurately known.

"I want to report to you, friends, that my imprisonment here has had the opposite of its intended effect. Instead of being squelched, the Message has actually prospered. All the soldiers here, and everyone else, too, found out that I'm in jail because of this Messiah. That piqued their curiosity, and now they've learned all about him. Not only that, but most of the followers of Jesus here have become more sure of themselves in the faith than ever before, speaking out fearlessly about God, about the Messiah . . . everything happening to me in this jail only serves to make Christ more accurately known, regardless of whether I live or die. They didn't shut me up; they gave me a pulpit! Alive, I'm Christ's messenger; dead, I'm his bounty. Life versus even more life! I can't lose." Philippians 1:12-14, 20-21 MSG

Teach me to trust.

"We felt we were doomed to die and saw how powerless we were to help ourselves; but that was good, for then we put everything into the hands of God, who alone could save us." II Corinthians 1:9 TLB

Prayer: "Thank you God for educating me. For loving me. For disciplining me. For treating me as your own dear child. Thank You for training me and for not spoiling me. Thank You for doing what you know is best for me".

Breathe: This too shall pass. God has a plan.

16 MORE THAN ENOUGH

My need - His sufficiency

I feel like a snow cone without ice, a bride without a groom, and clouds without the rain. Though surrounded by friends, I feel utterly alone. It is hot and dry. *Where are you, God? I cannot see you. I cannot hear you. I cannot feel your touch.*

At first, I had hope. *Just around the corner, there is an oasis for me,* but it is never there, just blazing sun and blistering sand. One mile, ten, a thousand, I trudge on no relief in sight. *I am not asking for much, God. Just a shady palm and cool water to quench my thirsty soul.*

I have stopped expecting. I have stopped believing. Does he know that I am alone? That I hurt and am afraid?

"Wherever you are, do you hear me, God? I have had enough. I quit!"

The setting sun kisses the day goodbye and I tremble in the darkness. Demonic darkness hisses, pointing a gnarled finger and mocking, "Nothing you do will ever be good enough. Of course, God has forgotten you. You do not see him. You do not hear him. You cannot feel his touch. You are alone, alone, alone."

Please somebody stop the pain, make it go away. No one does; because no one can. A rock for my pillow, burning sand for my bed, I toss, turn, and cry. Will I ever see green pastures again? Has God banished me to live out my days in this barren wilderness?

Sometime in the early morning hours, I drift into the blessed release of sleep. Hours later, I stir, aware even before I open my eyes that something has changed. A gentle breeze cools my brow.

I am not alone. I sense Him more than see Him. The accusing voice is gone, replaced with a soft whisper of hope. I acknowledge his presence, "My Lord and my God."

Fully awake, I drink deeply of the cool water he offers and it satisfies my soul. He holds my dusty face between his tough but tender hands. He turns it toward his own and I am lost in his eyes. He smiles, I smile. At last, my journey is at an end.

He wraps me in his strong arms and cradles me close. I feel safe in his embrace. He speaks and I listen hoping that his words will promise a tomorrow filled with wonder and joy. I wait to hear him say that my quota of sorrow has been filled, and I will never feel pain again.

What is this? The words he speaks are not at all, what I had hoped to hear. "Am I enough? If tomorrow is always as today, am I enough?"

I repeat His question; not sure I have understood, "If tomorrow is always as today, are you enough?" I pull away, eyes ablaze, and I spit my angry words like pointed bullets, "No! Absolutely no! You are not enough. I need lush pastures, morning mist, bubbling streams and caroling birds. I need a home to go home to, fresh strawberries, a baby's sweet smile, a soft pillow for my head". A tear trickles down my cheek, and he gently wipes it with his thumb. I begin to sob.

"You know what else I need, God? I need someone who understands, to help me carry my load. I need a friend who will love me and laugh at my silly jokes. A friend who will weep with me, and hold my hand and whisper, "You are mine. I love you. Do not be afraid, I am here. Do you understand, Lord? Do you understand what I need?"

"I believe I do," He smiles warmly, "what you need is me. I understand. I will carry your load; I will laugh at your silly jokes. I will cry with you, and then dry your tears. I will hold your hand in mine. When the storm is raging, I will shelter you safe. I will pull you close and whisper, 'Do not be afraid, I am here.' I will give you rest."

For a moment, He is quiet, and then he softly speaks once more, "No one can be everything you need. No one except me."

It's hot and dry. The desert wind blows, but there is an oasis ahead for me.

"Am I enough?" He whispers, arms outstretched. I feel like an icy-cold snow cone, a bride with her groom, gentle rain on a hot summer day.

"Yes, Lord. You are enough. You are more than enough for me."

"Desperate, I throw myself on him: He is my God!" Psalm 31:13-15 MSG

Breathe: This too shall pass. God has a plan.

17 SING TO ME

Lifting my voice heavenward, I whispered a plea that emitted from the depths of my ragged soul. My words, barely more than a whisper, spoken with the surrender that comes at the end of a long, hard battle. My beloved mother was walking her final mile. For four years, she had fought Metastatic Malignant Melanoma Stage IV. Now it appeared the cancer had won.

Tears coursing down my cheeks I plead, 'God of my life, grant me a song in my night. Please, sing to me, Lord. I'm listening!' Then He began to sing. I listened carefully hoping that the lyrics of his song would be filled with the promise of a tomorrow filled with only hope and joy. I listened for assurance that he would miraculously heal my mother this side of heaven. I waited to hear him sing that my quota of sorrow had been filled, and I would never feel pain again.

What's this? The words he sang were not at all, what I had hoped to hear. This cannot be! He is singing the wrong song. No, I do not want to hear these words. I struggled, longing to close my ears, to run from the words of his song.

The storm raged inside my heart, and then he spoke with calm authority.

"Peace! Be still!"

The tempest ceased, and a sweet peace settled over me. I laid my weary head once more upon his breast, and as I did, the realization came that the melody he sang kept perfect cadence with the beating of his heart. I felt comforted and soothed as his words washed over me with the healing balm of hope.

"This hour means something to me, too, my child," he sang. "I know you want to walk, I know you want to run, but little one this is one of those times when you need to let me carry you. I will, if you will let me. I will carry you."

"I feel so alone, Father."

Brushing the hair from my face, he sang, "I love you, and my tears were the first to fall when you learned of your mother's cancer. I have never left you, I have never forsaken you."

I wept then, great sobs shaking my body. "It hurts so much, dear Father; it . . . hurts . . . so . . . much. My spirit is wounded, and I cannot bear it."

Then he sang, "I am the refiner, purifying your soul as the finest of silver and gold. Let me do my work, dear child, and you will be to me an offering of righteousness. I will take your ashes and from them I will bring great beauty. I will change your sorrow into joy. I will clothe you with a garment of praise, instead of a spirit of despair. And, when I have done my work, you will be a planting for me, that I might be glorified."

"I'm so scared, Father. I cannot do this. I don't think I'm going to make it."

Gently, the words of his song, strong and tender, wrapped softly around my heart, "Do not be afraid. I am here. When you pass through the waters, I will be with you; and when you pass through the rivers, they will not sweep over. When you walk through the fire you will not be burned; the flames will not set you ablaze."

"I can't see the path - I don't know which way to go. Nothing is the same. I don't think life will ever be normal again."

"I will give you a new normal, my child. I have a plan. Will you let me redeem this sorrow in your life? Let me bring good out of the great pain you have borne?" I tried to pull from the security of his arms, shouting, "Bring good out of my pain? If you are love; why did you let this happen in the first place?"

I struggled, hoping all the while that He . . . would . . . not . . . let . . . me . . . go.

Tenderly he pulled me back into the safety of his embrace, and he sang, "Suffering is part of the human experience. Because I love, I will bring good out of your sorrow. I am not the author of everything that happens in this world, but I am the Master. If you will allow me, I will touch you deeper than your deepest hurts."

"It's dark, and I am so afraid."

"I know the storm is raging and the night is black, but I'm in the darkness - it is light to me. I will command my lovingkindness in the daytime, and in the night my song shall be with you."

"I want to trust. I want to believe, but, God, I don't understand."

"I know you don't. My grace will support you even when you cannot understand it. You think it is all over, but I have just begun. When you are through this dark night, you will be able to serve me in ways you never imagined, before this trial of your faith. Endurance is not just the ability to bear a hard thing, but to turn it into glory. You may not understand my ways but, look at me; can you see my love for you, written in the tears on my face?" "Oh, Jesus help me!" He did. His song became my own.

Breathe: This too shall pass. God has a plan

ABOUT THE AUTHOR

Ronda Knuth lives in Lakewood, CO, with her husband Rob. She is a mother of four, grandmother of four, and mother in love of three.

Ronda is a freelance writer and a regular contributor to the Network 211.com, with many articles published on their Global Christian Center website.

She is also a regular contributor to The Way.co.uk in the United Kingdom, on their subscription service daily devotionals; published online.

Ronda has spoken at numerous area retreats, luncheons, civic and church groups. She has appeared on numerous radio and television programs, including, "The 700 Club," "Sally Jesse Raphael," "Phil Donahue," and "Inside Edition".

Her first published book, When Memory Fades: Sunrise Stories from Real People is now available in both print and Kindle editions from Amazon.com

Learn more about Ronda at her website:

http://rondasrestingplace.net

The *Sunrise Senior Living Company* recognized her dedication, to making the facility at Pinehurst, Denver, CO, residents' lives the happiest and best they can be. When presented with the

'Joy in Service Award'

she asked why she was given an award for simply loving?"

BREATHE: THIS TOO SHALL PASS!

THE END

RONDA KNUTH

Made in the USA
Monee, IL
08 April 2025

15305679R00049